T0302859

Look and See 1

Susannah Reed

NATIONAL GEOGRAPHIC
LEARNING

Australia • Brazil • Mexico • Singapore • United Kingdom • United States

Scope and Sequence

What's your name? p. 4 — *What's your name?* *My name's ...*

Unit		Words	Structure	Value	Letters and Sounds/ Numbers	Content Connections: Video	Content Connections: Project
1 Hello! p. 5		*Hello!* *Goodbye.* *Say hello.* *Wave goodbye.* *Stand up.* *Sit down.* *Open your book.* *Close your book.*	*How are you?* *I'm fine, thank you.*	Make friends.	Aa /æ/	Social Science How do people say hello around the world?	A puppet
2 School p. 11		*school* *apron* *bag* *chair* *crayon* *pencil* *table*	*What's this?* *It's a pencil.*	Look after your things.	1, 2	Social Science How are classrooms different around the world?	A pencil holder
3 Colours p. 17		*paint* *blue* *green* *orange* *purple* *red* *yellow*	*What colour is the book?* *It's red.*	Be creative.	Ee /e/	Art What happens when we mix primary colours?	A squish painting
4 Toys p. 23		*train* *ball* *bus* *car* *doll* *puppet* *teddy bear*	*I've got a ball.*	Share your toys.	3, 4	Social Science What land transportation do we use?	A bus collage
5 Let's move! p. 29		*body* *arms* *feet* *hands* *head* *legs* *tummy*	*Touch your head.* *Move your hands.*	Be active.	Ii /ɪ/	Music, PE What are different ways to dance?	A shaker

		Words	Structure	Value	Letters and Sounds/ Numbers	Content Connections: Video	Content Connections: Project
6 **Food** p. 35		*apple* *banana* *biscuit* *carrot* *milk* *orange* *water*	*I like oranges.* *Me, too!*	Choose healthy food.	5, 6	Science How do plants grow?	An apple tree book
7 **My family** p. 41		*photo* *brother* *dad* *grandma* *grandpa* *mum* *sister*	*This is my mum.*	Be kind to your family.	Oo /ɒ/	Science Do animals live in families?	A photo frame
8 **On the farm** p. 47		*chicken* *cat* *cow* *dog* *goat* *horse* *sheep*	*Is it a cow?* *No, it isn't.* *Is it a horse?* *Yes, it is.*	Look after animals.	7, 8	Science What do we get from farm animals?	A paper-plate sheep
9 **My clothes** p. 53		*hat* *jacket* *shoes* *shorts* *socks* *T-shirt* *black, brown, white*	*My T-shirt is orange.* *My shorts are red.*	Dress yourself.	Uu /ʌ/	Social Science How is wool made into clothes?	A wool jumper
10 **Outside** p. 59		*frog* *bird* *fish* *flower* *leaf* *rainbow* *tree*	*How many birds?* *Four birds.*	Explore outside.	9, 10	Science What animals use camouflage?	A camouflaged animal picture

Girls shaking hands at school, Bangladesh

STRUCTURE: *What's your name? My name's Jian.*

1 Look and see. **2** TR: 0.1 Listen and say. **3** TR: 0.2 Listen and sing. **4** TR: 0.3 Sing and do.

UNIT 1

Hello!

Happy children at school, Mongolia

LESSON 1

NEW WORDS: *Hello!, Goodbye.*

1 Look and see. **2** SC: 1 Watch. **3** TR: 1.1 Listen and say. **4** TR: 1.2 Listen and do.

A girl waving goodbye, Bulgaria

LESSON 2

NEW WORDS: *Say hello. Wave goodbye. Stand up. Sit down. Open your book. Close your book.*

1 TR: 1.3 Listen and point. **2** TR: 1.4 Listen and do. **3** TR: 1.5 Listen again and do.

LESSON 3

STRUCTURE: *How are you? I'm fine, thank you.*

1 TR: 1.6 Listen and point. **2** TR: 1.7 Listen and say. **3** Play and say.

Smiling children, Australia

Think! Value

Make friends.

LESSON 4

SONG AND VALUE: *Make friends.*

1 TR: 1.8 Listen and point. **2** TR: 1.9 Listen and sing. **3** TR: 1.10 Sing and do. **4** Stick.

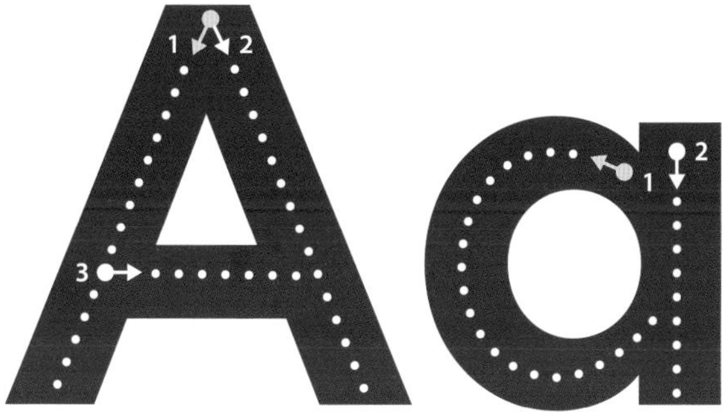

A → a

Aa → 

LESSON 5

LETTERS AND SOUNDS: Aa, /æ/

1 TR: 1.11 Listen and point. **2** TR: 1.12 Listen. Trace and say. **3** TR: 1.13 Listen and chant. **4** Draw and say.

Inupiaq children saying hello, Alaska, USA

LESSON 6

VIDEO Content Word: *world*

1 Look and see. **2** SC: 2 Watch. **3** SC: 2 Watch and say.

LESSON 7

PROJECT

1 Make.

UNIT 2 School

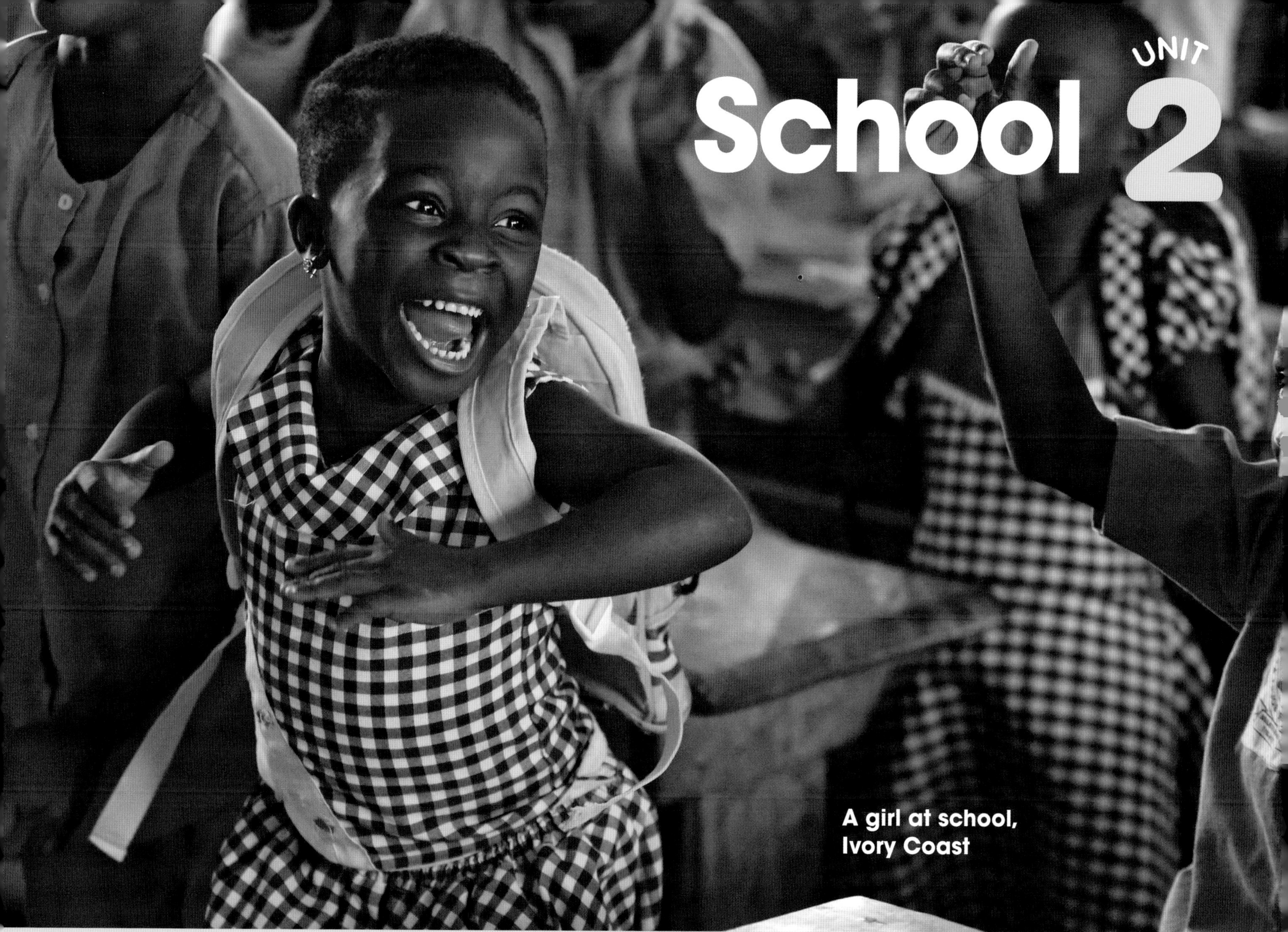

A girl at school, Ivory Coast

LESSON 1

NEW WORD: *school*

1 Look and see. **2** SC: 3 Watch. **3** TR: 2.1 Listen and say. **4** TR: 2.2 Listen and do.

Boy at school, Guatemala

LESSON 2

NEW WORDS: *apron, bag, chair, crayon, pencil, table*

1 TR: 2.3 Listen and point. **2** TR: 2.4 Listen and say. **3** TR: 2.5 Listen and chant.

LESSON 3

STRUCTURE: *What's this? It's a pencil.*

1 TR: 2.6 Listen and point. **2** TR: 2.7 Listen and say. **3** Play and say.

Boys reading together, UAE

Think! Value

Look after your things.

LESSON 4

SONG AND VALUE: *Look after your things.*

1 TR: 2.8 Listen and point. **2** TR: 2.9 Listen and sing. **3** TR: 2.10 Sing and do. **4** Stick.

1 

2 

LESSON 5 **NUMBERS:** 1, 2

1 TR: 2.11 Listen and point. **2** TR: 2.12 Listen. Trace and say. **3** TR: 2.13 Listen and chant. **4** Draw and count.

Girls and boys at school, Vietnam

Children reading at school, Georgia

LESSON 6

VIDEO **Content Words:** *classroom, different, fun, teacher*

1 Look and see. **2** SC: 4 Watch. **3** SC: 4 Watch and say.

LESSON 7

PROJECT

1 Make.

Colours

UNIT 3

A girl covered in paint

LESSON 1

NEW WORD: *paint*

1 Look and see. **2** SC: 5 Watch. **3** TR: 3.1 Listen and say. **4** TR: 3.2 Listen and do.

red	orange	yellow	green	blue	purple

LESSON 2

NEW WORDS: *blue, green, orange, purple, red, yellow*

1 TR: 3.3 Listen and point. **2** TR: 3.4 Listen and say. **3** TR: 3.5 Listen and chant.

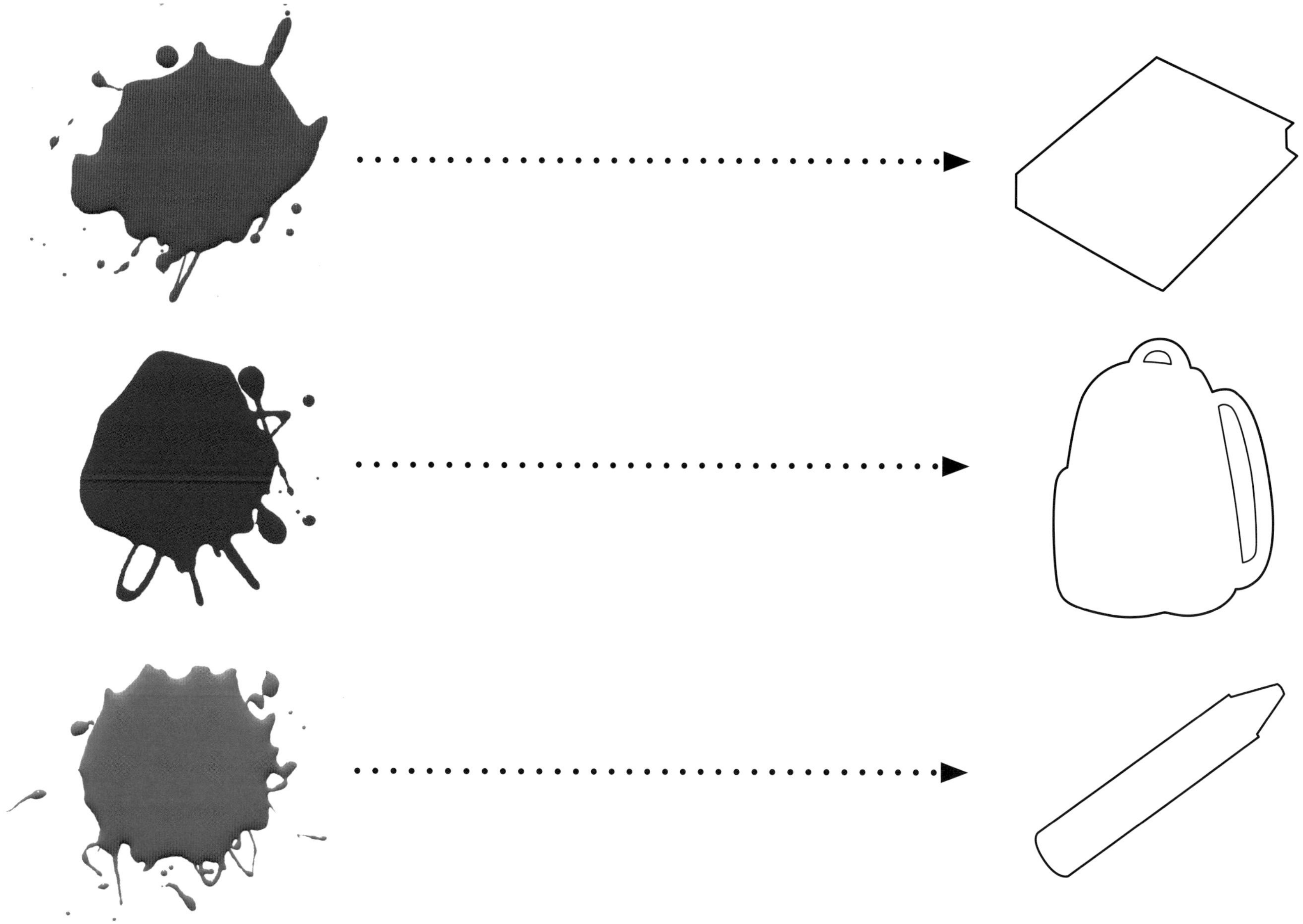

LESSON 3

STRUCTURE: *What colour is the book? It's red.*

1 TR: 3.6 Listen and point. Draw. **2** TR: 3.7 Listen and say. **3** Colour and say.

A child with artwork, Brazil

Think! Value

Be creative.

LESSON 4

SONG AND VALUE: *Be creative.*

1 TR: 3.8 Listen and point. **2** TR: 3.9 Listen and sing. **3** TR: 3.10 Sing and do. **4** Stick.

Ee

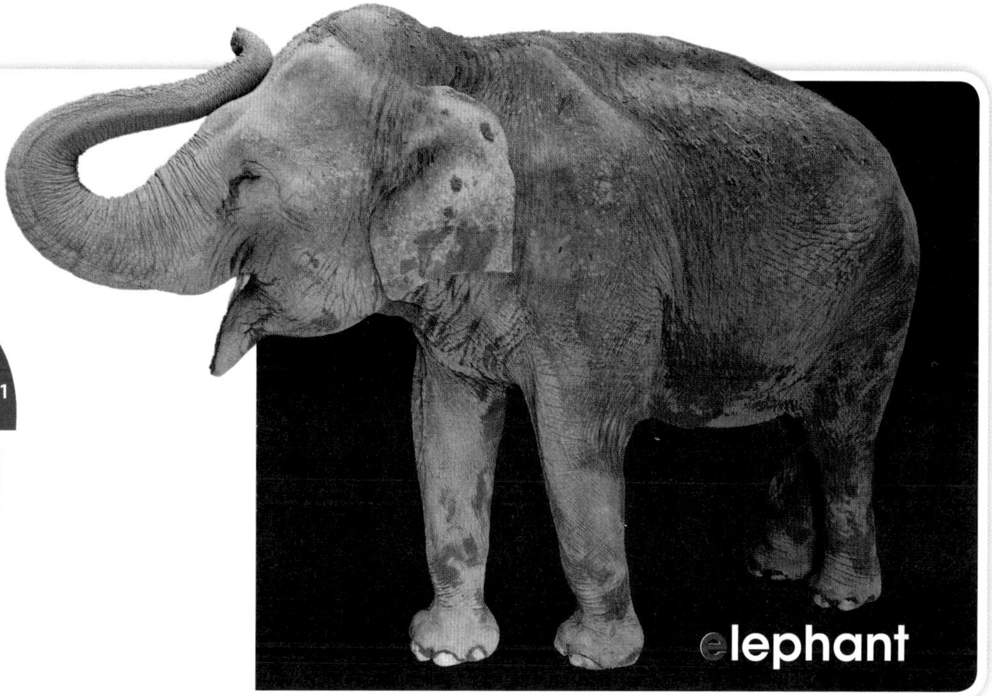

E e

Ee

LESSON 5

LETTERS AND SOUNDS: Ee, /e/

1 TR: 3.11 Listen and point. **2** TR: 3.12 Listen. Trace and say. **3** TR: 3.13 Listen and chant. **4** Draw and say.

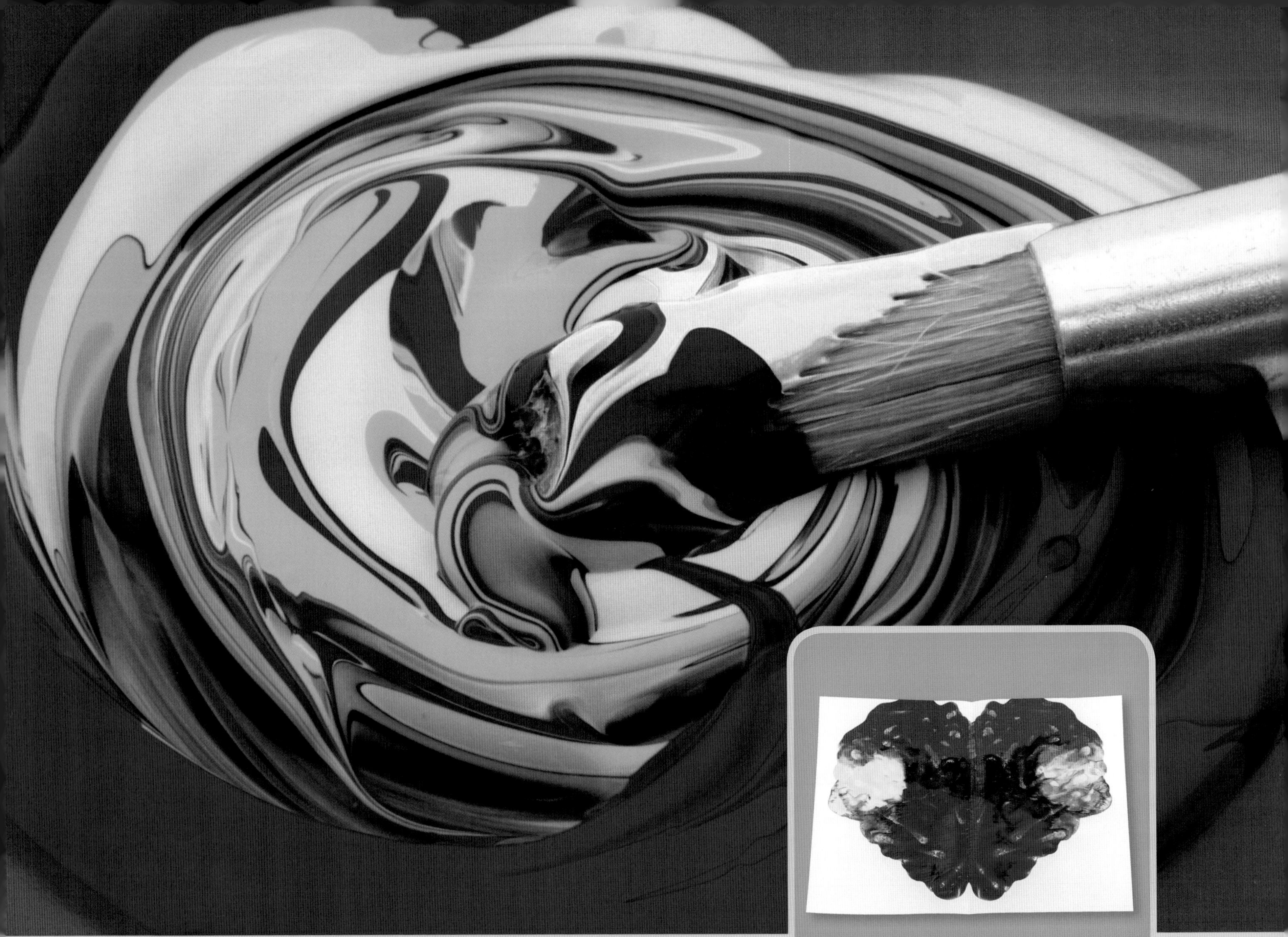

LESSON 6

VIDEO **Content Words:** *make, picture*

1 Look and see. **2** SC: 6 Watch. **3** SC: 6 Watch and say.

LESSON 7

PROJECT

1 Make.

UNIT 4 Toys

A train show at the New York Botanical Garden, USA

LESSON 1

NEW WORD: *train*

1 Look and see. **2** SC: 7 Watch. **3** TR: 4.1 Listen and say. **4** TR: 4.2 Listen and do.

A boy with his toy car, UAE

LESSON 2

NEW WORDS: *ball, bus, car, doll, puppet, teddy bear*

1 TR: 4.3 Listen and point. **2** TR: 4.4 Listen and say. **3** TR: 4.5 Listen and chant.

LESSON 3

STRUCTURE: *I've got a ball.*

1 TR: 4.6 Listen and point. **2** TR: 4.7 Listen and say. **3** Play and say.

Boys playing with toy cars, South Africa

Girls playing with toys, China

Think! Value

Share your toys.

LESSON 4

SONG AND VALUE: *Share your toys.*

1 TR: 4.8 Listen and point. **2** TR: 4.9 Listen and sing. **3** TR: 4.10 Sing and do. **4** Stick.

3 

4 

LESSON 5

NUMBERS: 3, 4

1 TR: 4.11 Listen and point. **2** TR: 4.12 Listen. Trace and say. **3** TR: 4.13 Listen and chant. **4** Draw and count.

Trains, buses and cars, Malaysia

LESSON 6

VIDEO **Content Words:** *big, pink, small*

1 Look and see. **2** SC: 8 Watch. **3** SC: 8 Watch, point and say.

LESSON 7

PROJECT

1 Make.

UNIT 5

Let's move!

A girl climbing, England

LESSON 1

NEW WORD: *body*

1 Look and see. **2** SC: 9 Watch. **3** TR: 5.1 Listen and say. **4** TR: 5.2 Listen and do.

LESSON 2

NEW WORDS: *arms, feet, hands, head, legs, tummy*

1 TR: 5.3 Listen and point. **2** TR: 5.4 Listen and say. **3** TR: 5.5 Listen and chant.

touch

move

LESSON 3

STRUCTURE: *Touch your head. Move your hands.*

1 TR: 5.6 Listen and point. **2** TR: 5.7 Listen and say. **3** Play and say.

Children dancing together, China

Think! Value

Be active.

LESSON 4

SONG AND VALUE: *Be active.*

1 Look and see. **2** TR: 5.8 Listen and do. **3** TR: 5.9 Listen and sing. **4** Stick.

LESSON 5

LETTERS AND SOUNDS: Ii, /ɪ/

1 TR: 5.10 Listen and point. **2** TR: 5.11 Listen. Trace and say. **3** TR: 5.12 Listen and chant. **4** Draw and say.

Dancers at a festival, Mexico

LESSON 6

VIDEO **Content Words:** *clap, dance, left, right, stomp*

1 Look and see. **2** SC: 10 Watch. **3** SC: 10 Watch and do.

LESSON 7

PROJECT

1 Make.

UNIT 6 Food

An apple orchard, USA

LESSON 1

NEW WORD: *apple*

1 Look and see. **2** SC: 11 Watch. **3** TR: 6.1 Listen and say. **4** TR: 6.2 Listen and do.

LESSON 2

NEW WORDS: *banana, biscuit, carrot, milk, orange, water*

1 TR: 6.3 Listen and point. **2** TR: 6.4 Listen and say. **3** TR: 6.5 Listen and chant.

LESSON 3

STRUCTURE: *I like oranges. Me, too!*

1 TR: 6.6 Listen and point. **2** TR: 6.7 Listen and say. **3** Colour and say.

A fruit market, Indonesia

Think! Value

Choose healthy food.

LESSON 4

SONG AND VALUE: *Choose healthy food.*

1 TR: 6.8 Listen and point. **2** TR: 6.9 Listen and sing. **3** TR: 6.10 Sing and do. **4** Stick.

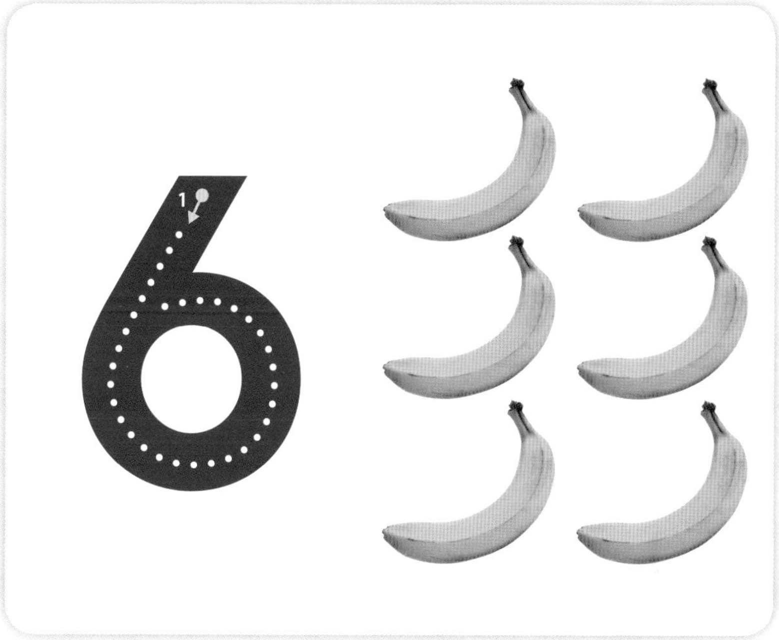

5

6

LESSON 5

NUMBERS: 5, 6

1 TR: 6.11 Listen and point. **2** TR: 6.12 Listen. Trace and say. **3** TR: 6.13 Listen and chant. **4** Draw and count.

LESSON 6

VIDEO **Content Words:** *grow, plant, seed, tree*

1 Look and see. **2** SC: 12 Watch. **3** SC: 12 Watch, point and say.

LESSON 7

PROJECT

1 Make.

UNIT 7

My family

A family celebration, China

LESSON 1

NEW WORD: *photo*

1 Look and see. **2** SC: 13 Watch. **3** TR: 7.1 Listen and say. **4** TR: 7.2 Listen and do.

LESSON 2

NEW WORDS: *brother, dad, grandma, grandpa, mum, sister*

1 TR: 7.3 Listen and point. **2** TR: 7.4 Listen and say. **3** TR: 7.5 Listen and chant.

LESSON 3

STRUCTURE: *This is my mum.*

1 TR: 7.6 Listen and point. **2** TR: 7.7 Listen and say. **3** Draw and say.

A boy and his grandma, Slovakia

Think! Value

Be kind to your family.

LESSON 4

SONG AND VALUE: *Be kind to your family.*

1 TR: 7.8 Listen and point. **2** TR: 7.9 Listen and sing. **3** TR: 7.10 Sing and do. **4** Stick.

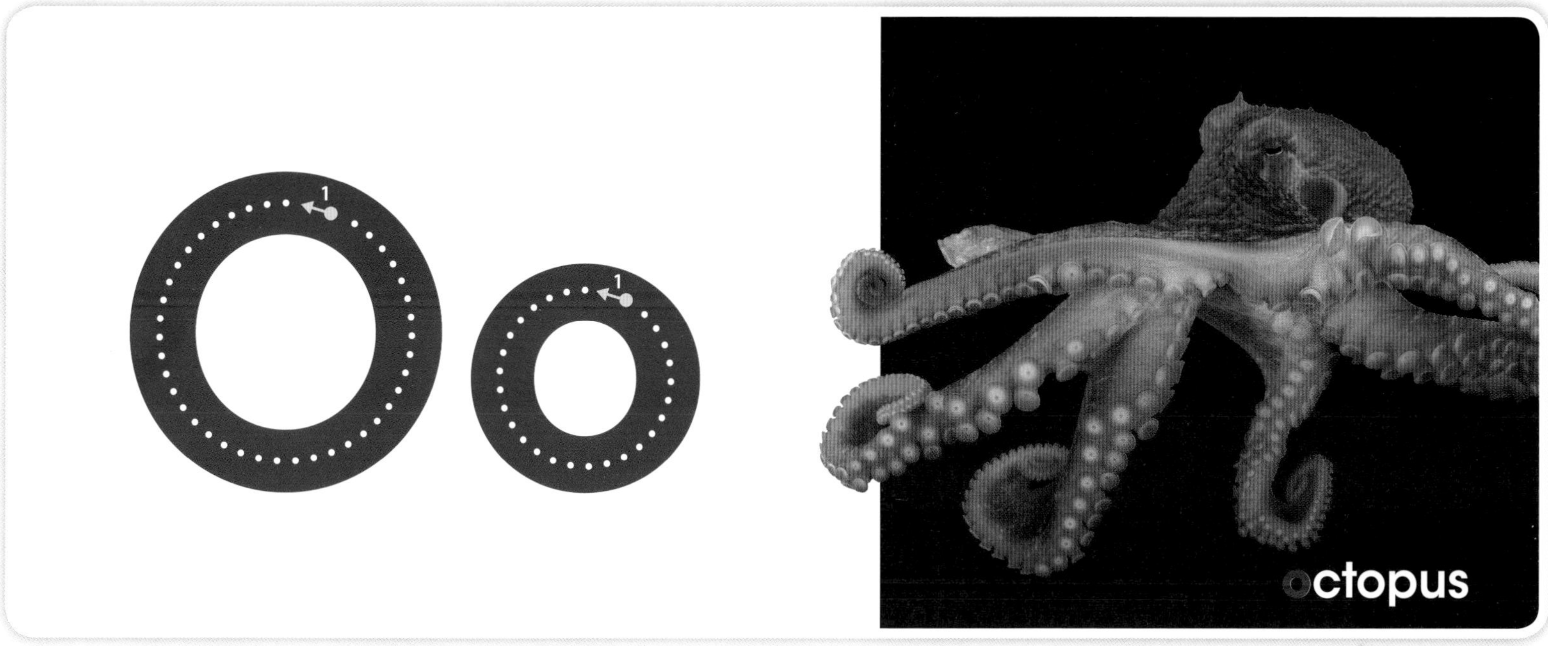

LESSON 5

LETTERS AND SOUNDS: Oo, /ɒ/

1 TR: 7.11 Listen and point. **2** TR: 7.12 Listen. Trace and say. **3** TR: 7.13 Listen and chant. **4** Draw and say.

Lions and elephants, Kenya

LESSON 6

VIDEO **Content Words:** *baby, cub, lion*

1 Look and see. **2** SC: 14 Watch. **3** SC: 14 Watch, point and say.

LESSON 7

PROJECT

1 Make.

UNIT 8

On the farm

Chickens leaving their coop, USA

LESSON 1

NEW WORD: *chicken*

1 Look and see. **2** SC: 15 Watch. **3** TR: 8.1 Listen and say. **4** TR: 8.2 Listen and do.

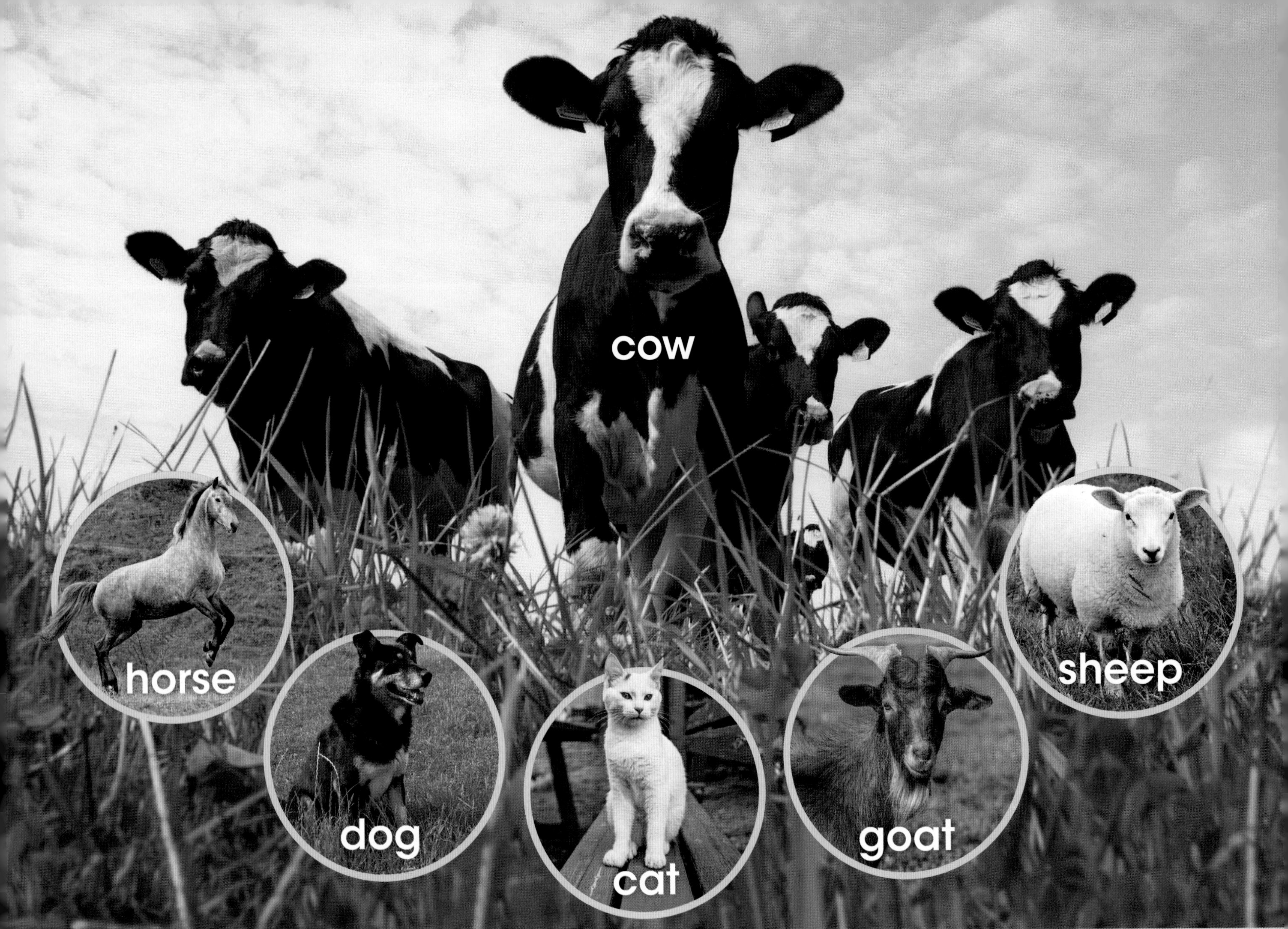

LESSON 2

NEW WORDS: *cat, cow, dog, goat, horse, sheep*

1 TR: 8.3 Listen and point. **2** TR: 8.4 Listen and say. **3** TR: 8.5 Listen and chant.

LESSON 3

STRUCTURE: *Is it a cow? No, it isn't. Is it a horse? Yes, it is.*

1 TR: 8.6 Listen and point. **2** TR: 8.7 Listen and say. **3** Play and say.

A boy feeding a horse, Australia

A girl feeding a lamb, USA

Think! Value

Look after animals.

LESSON 4

SONG AND VALUE: *Look after animals.*

1 TR: 8.8 Listen and point. **2** TR: 8.9 Listen and sing. **3** TR: 8.10 Sing and do. **4** Stick.

7 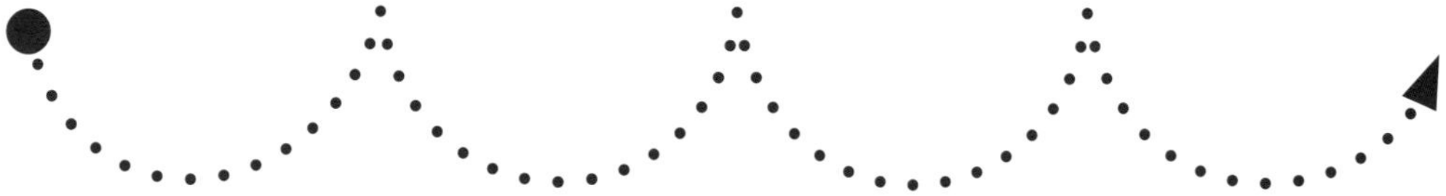 

8  

LESSON 5

NUMBERS: 7, 8

1 TR: 8.11 Listen and point. **2** TR: 8.12 Listen. Trace and say. **3** TR: 8.13 Listen and chant. **4** Draw and count.

LESSON 6

VIDEO **Content Words:** *egg, wool*

1 Look and see. **2** SC: 16 Watch. **3** SC: 16 Watch, point and say.

LESSON 7

PROJECT

1 Make.

UNIT 9 My clothes

Children with hats, Peru

LESSON 1

NEW WORD: *hat*

1 Look and see. **2** SC: 17 Watch. **3** TR: 9.1 Listen and say. **4** TR: 9.2 Listen and do.

Girls at an ice festival, South Korea

LESSON 2

NEW WORDS: *jacket, shoes, shorts, socks, T-shirt; black, brown, white*

1 TR: 9.3 Listen and point. **2** TR: 9.4 Listen and say. **3** TR: 9.5 Listen and chant.

LESSON 3

STRUCTURE: *My T-shirt is orange. My shorts are red.*

1 TR: 9.6 Listen and point. **2** TR: 9.7 Listen and say. **3** Play and say.

A boy with a yellow jacket, Germany

A girl with white shoes, UK

Think! Value

Dress yourself.

LESSON 4

SONG AND VALUE: *Dress yourself.*

1 TR: 9.8 Listen and point. **2** TR: 9.9 Listen and sing. **3** TR: 9.10 Sing and do. **4** Stick.

Uu

U u

Uu

LESSON 5

LETTERS AND SOUNDS: Uu, /ʌ/

1 TR: 9.11 Listen and point. **2** TR: 9.12 Listen. Trace and say. **3** TR: 9.13 Listen and chant. **4** Draw and say.

LESSON 6

VIDEO **Content Words:** *jumper, scarf, wool*

1 Look and see. **2** SC: 18 Watch. **3** SC: 18 Watch, point and say.

LESSON 7

PROJECT

1 Make.

Outside

UNIT 10

Dumpy tree frogs in the rain, Indonesia

LESSON 1

NEW WORD: *frog*

1 Look and see. **2** SC: 19 Watch. **3** TR: 10.1 Listen and say. **4** TR: 10.2 Listen and do.

LESSON 2

NEW WORDS: *bird, fish, flower, leaf, rainbow, tree*

1 TR: 10.3 Listen and point. **2** TR: 10.4 Listen and say. **3** TR: 10.5 Listen and chant.

LESSON 3

STRUCTURE: *How many birds? Four birds.*

1 TR: 10.6 Listen and point. **2** TR: 10.7 Listen and say. **3** Play and say.

Three parrots, Costa Rica

Think! Value

Explore outside.

LESSON 4

SONG AND VALUE: *Explore outside.*

1 TR: 10.8 Listen and point. **2** TR: 10.9 Listen and sing. **3** TR: 10.10 Sing and do. **4** Stick.

9

10

LESSON 5

NUMBERS: 9, 10

1 TR: 10.11 Listen and point. **2** TR: 10.12 Listen. Trace and say. **3** TR: 10.13 Listen and chant. **4** Draw and count.

LESSON 6

VIDEO **Content Words:** *insect, lizard*

1 Look and see. **2** SC: 20 Watch. **3** SC: 20 Watch, point and say.

LESSON 7

PROJECT

1 Make.

UNIT 1

Hello!

Hello, my friend.
How are you?
I'm fine, thank you.
I'm fine, too.

[Chorus]
Let's say hello!
Let's make friends.
Let's make friends together.

Hello, my friend.
How are you?
I'm fine, thank you.
I'm fine, too.

[Chorus]

UNIT 2

School

What's this?
It's a book.
It's my book.
My nice, new book!

Look after your book.
Look after your things.

What's this?
It's a pencil.
It's my pencil.
My nice, new pencil!

Look after your pencil.
Look after your things.

UNIT 3

Colours

Here is red and yellow, too.
Here is green and blue.

[Chorus]
Look at the colours,
beautiful colours!
What colours can you see?

Here is green and yellow, too.
Here is red and blue.

[Chorus]

UNIT 4

Toys

I've got a car.
And I've got a car.
Two cars - one and two.
One for me and one for you.

Let's share the cars.
Let's share the toys!

I've got a ball.
And I've got a ball.
Two balls - one and two.
One for me and one for you.

Let's share the balls.
Let's share the toys!

UNIT 5

Let's move!

Move your arms.
Move your hands.
Up and down,
arms and hands.

[Chorus]
Let's be active:
one, two, three!
Move your body.
Move with me!

Touch your legs.
Touch your feet.
Hands down
and touch your feet.

[Chorus]

UNIT 6

Food

I like apples.
I like oranges.
I like bananas, too.

[Chorus]
Look at the food.
It's healthy food.
Food for me and you.

I like bananas.
I like apples.
I like oranges, too.

[Chorus]

UNIT 8

On the farm

What's this? Is it a horse?
Yes, it is. It's a horse.
It's my horse, Maxi.
Here you are, Maxi.
This is for you.

Look after your horse.
Look after animals.

What's this? Is it a goat?
No, it isn't. It's a lamb.
It's my lamb, Suzy.
Here you are, Suzy.
This is for you.

Look after your lamb.
Look after animals.

UNIT 7

My family

Hello, Grandma. This is for you.
This is for me?
Oh, thank you! Thank you!
A nice surprise for me.

[Chorus]
Be kind to your family.
All your family.

Hello, Grandpa. This is for you.
A hug for me?
Oh, thank you! Thank you!
A nice, big hug for me.

[Chorus]

UNIT 9

My clothes

I've got a jacket.
Look at my jacket.
My jacket is yellow.

Put on your jacket,
your yellow jacket.
Dress yourself today.

I've got two shoes.
Look at my shoes.
My shoes are white.

Put on your shoes,
your white shoes.
Dress yourself today.

UNIT 10

Outside

[Chorus]
Come outside.
Explore outside.
Explore outside with me!

Look at the birds.
How many birds?
Three birds – one, two, three.

[Chorus]

Look at the flowers.
How many flowers?
Three flowers – one, two, three.

Aa

alligator

Bb

beaver

Cc

camel

Dd

duck

Ii

iguana

Jj

jaguar

Kk

kangaroo

Ll

lion

Qq

quail

Rr

reindeer

Ss

seal

Tt

tiger

Uu

umbrellabird

Ee

elephant

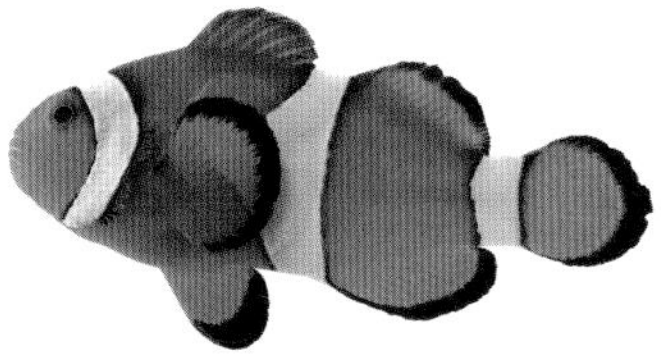

Ff

fish

Gg

gorilla

Hh

hippo

Mm

monkey

Nn

numbat

Oo

octopus

Pp

panda

Vv

vulture

Ww

wolf

Xx

fo**x**

Yy

yak

Zz

zebra

CREDITS

PHOTOS: 2 (t) © Jan Zammit; (mt) Courtesy of Frank DeJongh/UNICEF; (m) joey333/iStock/Getty Images; (mb) Xinhua News Agency/Getty Images; (b) Look/Alamy Stock Photo; **3** (t) © Inge Johnsson; (mt) © John Stanmeyer; (m) © Charlie Hamilton James/National Geographic Image Collection; (mb) Otographer/Pilar Olivares/Reuters; (b) lovethephoto/Alamy Stock Photo; **4** Courtesy of UNICEF/UNI138867/Haque; **5** © Jan Zammit; **6** (tl) Kativ/E+/Getty Images; (tr) David Hanson/Aurora Photos; (bl) paultarasenko/Shutterstock.com; (bm) Tetra Images, LLC/Alamy Stock Photo; (br) AustinandAugust/Shutterstock.com; (background) praetorianphoto/iStock/Getty Images; **8** Ulla Lohmann/Robert Harding Library; **9** (t) Joel Sartore/National Geographic Image Collection; (b) reptiles4all/Shutterstock.com; **10** Design Pics Inc/Alamy Stock Photo; (project) © 2021 Cengage; **11** Courtesy of Frank DeJongh/UNICEF; **12** (tl) ZouZou/Shutterstock.com; (tm) iprachenko/Shutterstock.com; (tr) Mega Pixel/Shutterstock.com; (m) John Kasawa/Shutterstock.com; (b) Juris Kraulis/Alamy Stock Photo; (background) Keith Levit/Perspectives/Getty Images; **13** (tl) tavizta/Shutterstock.com; (tm) chalrumpon onnongwa/Shutterstock.com; (tr) daizuoxin/Shutterstock.com; (bl) Natalya Erofeeva/Shutterstock.com; (br) AlexKrul/Shutterstock.com; (background) PowerUp/Shutterstock.com; **14** © Annie Griffiths; (inset) Westend61/Getty Images; **15** (t) Sergiy Tryapitsyn/Alamy Stock Photo; (m) Brian A Jackson/Shutterstock.com; (b) recebin/Shutterstock.com; **16** (t) Xinhua/eyevine/Redux; (b) Vano Shlamov/AFP/Getty Images; (project) © 2021 Cengage; **17** joey333/iStock/Getty Images; **18** Mark Mawson/Stone/Getty Images; **19** (all) irin-k/Shutterstock.com; **20** © Children at Risk Foundation; **21** (t) Joel Sartore/National Geographic Image Collection; (b) Andre Klopper/Shutterstock.com; **22** SasPartout/Shutterstock.com; (project) © 2021 Cengage; **23** Xinhua News Agency/Getty Images; **24** (tl) Sintez/iStock/Getty Images; (tr) Dorling Kindersley ltd/Alamy Stock Photo; (ml) CykOtie/Shutterstock.com; (mr) Mega Pixel/Shutterstock.com; (b) kyoshino/iStock/Getty Images; (background) Celia Peterson/Getty Images; **26** (l) AfriPics.com/Alamy Stock Photo; (r) John Warburton-Lee Photography/Alamy Stock Photo; **27** (t) Twin Design/Shutterstock.com; (m) Chayapon Bootboonneam/EyeEm/Getty Images; (r) Mega Pixel/Shutterstock.com; **28** Nikada/iStock Unreleased/Getty Images; (project) © 2021 Cengage; (l) Layland Masuda/Moment/Getty Images; (ml) Pongnaret Palamon/Shutterstock.com; (mr) paulaphoto/Shutterstock.com; (r) FotoAndalucia/Shutterstock.com; **29** lovethephoto/Alamy Stock Photo; **30** Alison Crane Photography/Moment/Getty Images; **31** (tl) Westend61 GmbH/Alamy Stock Photo; (tml) Dave King/Dorling Kindersley/Getty Images; (tmr) Werli Francois/Alamy Stock Photo; (tr) Karen Anderson/Moment Open/Getty Images; (bl) Apichet Chakreeyarut/Alamy Stock Photo; (bml) ViewStock/Getty Images; (bmr) sarahwolfephotography/Moment/Getty Images; (br) Maisie Paterson/Tetra images/Getty Images; (background) natrot/Shutterstock.com; **32** Philipp Engelhorn/laif/Redux; **33** (t) Joel Sartore/National Geographic Photo Ark/National Geographic Image Collection; (b) Rosa Jay/Shutterstock.com; **34** Larry Dale Gordon/The Image Bank/Getty Images; (project) © 2021 Cengage; **35** © Inge Johnsson; **36** (t) pidjoe/istock/Getty Images; (ml) Cheers Group/Shutterstock.com; (mm) Sergey Ivanychev/EyeEm/Getty Images; (mr) Tarasyuk Igor/Shutterstock.com; (b) Jiri Hera/Shutterstock.com; (background) Johanna Parkin/Photolibrary/Getty Images; **37** (tl) gu min/Shutterstock.com; (tm) sta/Shutterstock.com; (tr) PaulGrecaud/iStock/Getty Images; (bl) Tania Bertoni/Shutterstock.com; (bm) gowithstock/Shutterstock.com; (br) abimages/Shutterstock.com; (background) weedezign/Shutterstock.com; **38** brytta/iStock/Getty Images; **39** (tl) Cheers Group/Shutterstock.com; (tr) Sergey Ivanychev/EyeEm/Getty Images; (m) Anna Kucherova/Shutterstock.com; (b) Peter Dazeley/Photographer's Choice/Getty Images; **40** (tl) hacohob/Shutterstock.com; (tm) Valentina Razumova/Shutterstock.com; (tm/background) kzww/Shutterstock.com; (tr) Lumikk555/iStock/Getty Images; (bl) Robert Schneider/Alamy Stock photo; (br) lxefra/Moment/Getty Images; (project) © 2021 Cengage; **41** © John Stanmeyer; **42** subodhsathe/iStock/Getty Images; **44** (t) Halfpoint/iStock/Getty Images; (b) Jose Luis Pelaez Inc/DigitalVision/Getty Images; **45** (t, b) Joel Sartore/National Geographic Image Collection; **46** (t) David Lazar/Moment Select/Getty Images; (b) Anup Shah/Nature Picture Library; (project) © 2021 Cengage; imageBROKER/Alamy Stock Photo; **47** © Charlie Hamilton James/National Geographic Image Collection; **48** (l) pirita/Shutterstock.com; (ml) yuris/Shutterstock.com; (m) Matteo Fagiolino/Moment/Getty Images; (mr) MiaQu/Shutterstock.com; (r) IonelV/Shutterstock.com; (background) John Eveson/Minden Pictures; **49** (tl. tmlb) © Virginia Collins/EyeEm/Getty Images; (tmlt) © Sherjaca/Shutterstock.com; (tmr, trb) © Nicole Mulstay/Shutterstock.com; (trt) © Maika 777/Moment/Getty Images; (bl, brb) © chaoss/Shutterstock.com; (brt) © Skumer/Shutterstock.com; (background) © goory/Shutterstock.com; **50** (l) Belinda Dimarzio-Bryan/EyeEm/Getty Images; (r) Cavan Images/Cavan/Getty Images; **51** (tl) Kuznetsov Alexey/Shutterstock.com; (tr) Valentina_S/Shutterstock.com; (m) prochasson frederic/Shutterstock.com; (b) Chris Winsor/Moment/Getty Images; **52** (tl) Alfribeiro/iStock/Getty Images; (tr) PaulGrecaud/iStock/Getty Images; (b) Walter Bibikow/age fotostock/Robert Harding; (project) © 2021 Cengage; **53** Otographer/Pilar Olivares/Reuters; **54** (t) Iuliia Syrotina/Shutterstock.com; (ml) SakisPagonas/Shutterstock.com; (mr) New Africa/Shutterstock.com; (b) PhotoAlto/Laurence Mouton/PhotoAlto Agency RF Collections/Getty Images; (background) Menno Boermans/Cavan/Alamy Stock Photo; **55** (l) baona/iStock/Getty Images; (m) Watthano/Shutterstock.com; (r) Hogan Imaging/Shutterstock.com; (background) Alexlukin/Shutterstock.com; **56** (l) Westend61/Getty Images; (r) Dorling Kindersley/Getty Images; **57** (t) Joel Sartore/National Geographic Image Collection; (b) Ignacio Yufera/Biosphoto/Alamy Stock Photo; **58** (tl) berna namoglu/Shutterstock.com; (tr) Norbert Scanella/Robert Harding; (bl) elina nova/Shutterstock.com; (br) Halfpoint/iStock/Getty Images; (project) © Cengage; **59** Courtesy of Ajar Setiadi; **60** (l) rsooll/Shutterstock.com; (ml) KasperczakBohdan/Shutterstock.com; (mr) Brian Jannsen/Alamy Stock Photo; (r) Pavaphon Supanantananont/Shutterstock.com; (background) TomasSereda/iStock/Getty Images; **62** (t) Bence Mate/Nature Picture Library; (b) draasipos0323/iStock/Getty Images; **63** (tl) Fotofermer/Shutterstock.com; (tr) Barbol/Shutterstock.com; (m) Olhastock/Shutterstock.com; (b) Super Prin/Shutterstock.com; **64** (tl) robertharding/Image Bank Film/Getty Images; (tm) Discovod/Getty Images; (tr) National Geographic Image Collection; (b) Multi-bits/Image Bank Film/Getty Images; (project) © 2021 Cengage; **65** (l) Ulla Lohmann/Robert Harding Library; (r) Annie Griffiths/NGL Life as Lived; **66** (l) © Children at Risk Foundation; (r) John Warburton-Lee Photography/Alamy Stock Photo; **67** (l) Philipp Engelhorn/laif/Redux; (r) brytta/iStock/Getty Images; **68** (l) Jose Luis Pelaez Inc/DigitalVision/Getty Images; (r) Belinda Dimarzio-Bryan/EyeEm/Getty Images; **69** (l) Westend61/Getty Images; (r) Bence Mate/Nature Picture Library; **70** (all) Joel Sartore/National Geographic Photo Ark/National Geographic Image Collection; **71** (all) Joel Sartore/National Geographic Photo Ark/National Geographic Image Collection; **Back Cover** Joel Sartore/National Geographic Image Collection.

ILLUSTRATIONS: All mascot artwork created by Fabiana Faiallo; **7, 25, 61** Jill Dubin/Painted Words, Claire Easton; **8, 14, 20, 26, 32, 38, 43, 44, 50, 56, 62** Fabiana Faiallo; **19** Mary Rojas/Maggie Beyer Sprinzeles.